Volcanoes
Nature's Awesome Power

BY MARYANN DOBECK

TABLE OF CONTENTS

THIS BOOK BELONGS TO:

INTRODUCTION

A fiery stream of melted rock called **lava** shoots out of a mountaintop. Black clouds of ash choke the air. People who live nearby run away from the eruption. What phenomenon of nature are they fleeing from? It's a volcano!

Did you ever shake a bottle of soda and then remove the top? If so, you created something that erupts like a real volcano.

Many volcanoes will be erupting as you read this book—some on land, others deep beneath the sea.

Centuries ago, the native people of Hawaii witnessed volcanic eruptions, but they didn't know what caused them. So the Hawaiians made up stories to explain volcanic explosions on their islands. According to a Hawaiian myth, the goddess of volcanoes named Pele (PEH-lay) made mountains blow their top. When Pele got angry, look out! Fiery lava was her revenge.

Today, scientists know that forces of nature are the cause of volcanic eruptions. In this book, you'll learn about three different types of volcanoes and how they can create land as well as destroy it. As you read this book, imagine what it would be like to be a volcanologist who probes the dark mysteries of volcanoes.

It's a Fact

Volcanoes get their name from the island of Vulcano in the Mediterranean Sea. In ancient times, people thought that Vulcan, the god of fire, caused the eruptions on Vulcano.

THE INSIDE STORY OF VOLCANOES

To understand how volcanoes form, we need to look at how Earth is formed.

Earth is made up of four layers. The outer layer is the **crust**. Much like the shell of an egg, the crust surrounds the inner layers. Beneath the crust are the mantle, the outer core, and the inner core. The mantle is mostly solid rock about 1,800 miles (2,897 kilometers) thick. In some spots the temperature of the mantle reaches 9,000 degrees Fahrenheit (5,000 degrees Celsius)—hot enough to melt the solid rock into liquid rock called **magma**. The core of Earth is iron and nickel. The outer core is liquid. The inner core is solid.

Geologists (scientists who study Earth) believe that the entire crust and the upper part of the mantle are made up of about ten huge plates and six smaller plates. These plates are like large rafts that float on softer rock beneath them. The plates fit together somewhat like the pieces of a huge jigsaw puzzle.

They move as a result of built-up pressure from heat and gas below.

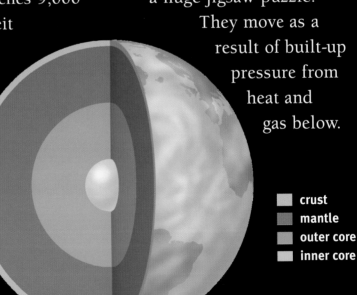

■ crust
■ mantle
■ outer core
■ inner core

The plates push into each other, pull away from each other, or slide past each other. The movement is very, very slow.

This plate theory is called **plate tectonics**. Most of the world's erupting volcanoes occur along the edges, or boundaries, of Earth's plates. The plate boundaries around the Pacific Ocean have many active volcanoes. This area is called the Ring of Fire.

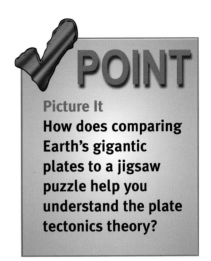

✓ POINT

Picture It
How does comparing Earth's gigantic plates to a jigsaw puzzle help you understand the plate tectonics theory?

Ring of Fire

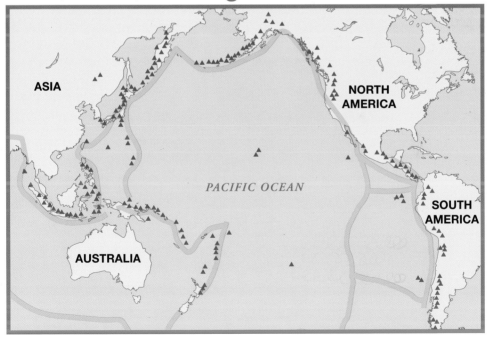

The Ring of Fire is the location of more than half the world's active volcanoes. Tectonic plate boundaries are shown on this map as orange lines.

A **volcano** is any opening on Earth where material from inside the planet—molten rock, debris, and steam—makes its way to the surface. What causes a volcanic eruption? Volcanoes erupt when pressures within Earth force magma to the surface. Magma collects deep underground in a magma chamber. Under pressure, the magma rises and bursts through the crust in weak spots called **vents**. When pressure on the magma subsides, the eruption stops. This is much like a tube of toothpaste that you squeeze. The harder you squeeze, the more toothpaste squirts out. When you stop squeezing, you stop the flow.

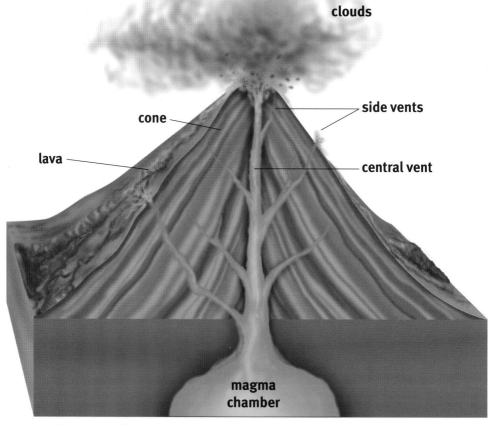

clouds

cone

side vents

lava

central vent

magma chamber

diagram of a volcanic eruption

Lava flows from the eruption of a Hawaiian volcano in 1999.

Three kinds of materials may erupt from a volcano: lava, tephra (rock fragments), and gases. Lava is magma that has reached the surface of a volcano. The terms pahoehoe (pah-HO-ee-hoh-ee) and aa (AH-ah) are Hawaiian words that describe the lava flow. *Aa* is thick. Like honey or molasses, it flows slowly down the slopes. *Pahoehoe* is thin and flows more quickly. When *pahoehoe* first erupts, get out of the way. This lava can outrun you!

All volcanoes release gases during an eruption. The pressure of the gas in the magma causes the eruption. Some volcanoes erupt with more than just lava. If the magma contains a lot of gas, it will burst out violently with rock fragments called pyroclastic (py-roh-KLAS-tik) materials. The pressure of the gas sends fragments of rock blasting out of the volcano. Some volcanoes alternate between eruptions of lava and eruptions of pyroclastic materials.

Sometimes a tall column of pyroclastic materials and gases collapses. It races down the slope of the volcano at dangerous speeds in what is called a **pyroclastic flow**. The speed of these flows can reach 120 miles per hour!

It's a Fact

The word *pyroclastic* comes from the Greek words for *fire* (pyro) and *broken* (klastos).

An eruption in 1980 creates a huge cloud of pyroclastic material above Mount St. Helens in Washington.

When a volcano erupts, it can spew out anything from fine particles of dust to huge blocks of rock as big as a house. This page shows several different kinds of volcanic matter.

Ash is small bits of lava.

Lapilli (la-PIH-ligh) are pebble-like bits of lava.

Blocks are large pieces of solid rock.

Bombs are large blobs of lava that harden as they spin through the air.

Do-It-Yourself Volcano

Here's how to make a model of an erupting volcano.
Do this in a sink, or a large pan. It will be fun, but messy.

YOU'LL NEED:

- A plastic soda bottle (the kind with a neck)
- Baking soda
- Dishwashing liquid
- Food coloring
- Vinegar
- Measuring spoons

WHAT TO DO:

1. Put 4 tablespoons of baking soda in the bottle.
2. Add some dishwashing liquid. (A few squirts should do it.)
3. Add a few drops of food coloring.
4. Add some vinegar, filling the bottle about one-third full. Now watch what happens!

From what you've learned in this chapter, answer the following questions:

- What part of a volcano does the bottle represent?
- Volcanoes need gas to erupt. What part of your experiment created the "gas"?
- Do you think your eruption was pyroclastic? Why or why not?

Volcanoes on the Ocean Floor

The tectonic plates on the ocean floor are thinner than the plates on land. This makes it easier for magma to create volcanoes on the ocean floor. New volcanoes are constantly being discovered in the South Pacific Ocean. Some of them rise more than a mile above the ocean floor. Yet their mountain peaks are still far below the surface of the sea.

Most volcanoes on the ocean floor do not rise above the ocean's surface. But one volcano off the coast of Iceland did break the surface. In 1963, this volcano formed a new island called Surtsey.

It's a Fact

A new Hawaiian island has been forming on the ocean floor. It is called Loihi (loh-EE-hee). Scientists say it could take up to one million years to reach the surface.

Surtsey Island

Volcanoes at Hot Spots

The largest volcanoes are above **hot spots**, areas of super-hot rock deep in Earth's mantle. At a hot spot, a plume of magma burns a hole in the plate. What happens next? You guessed it—a volcano!

The hot spots do not move, but the plates above them do. After one hot spot volcano forms, the plate above it moves. Then the same hot spot can create another volcano. In this way, a chain of volcanoes forms. Each of Hawaii's islands is actually the tip of an underwater volcano that formed over a hot spot in the Pacific Ocean. It took millions of years for the Hawaiian Islands to form. Hot spots also created the Galápagos Islands.

Hawaiian Islands from space

TYPES OF VOLCANOES

When you picture a volcano, what do you see? If you imagine a fountain of lava squirting out of a peak, you're partly right. You may be picturing a shield volcano. There are three common types of volcanoes: the stratovolcano, the cinder cone volcano, and the shield volcano. Geologists classify volcanoes based on their size, shape, and formation.

Stratovolcanoes

Stratovolcanoes usually have steep sides and a broad base. They are made of layers of lava as well as ash, cinders, and other pyroclastic materials. Quiet eruptions of lava follow explosive eruptions of pyroclastics. As layers of these materials pile up around the vent, they form a mountain thousands of feet above the base. Mount Fuji (FOO-jee) in Japan and Mount Shasta in California are stratovolcanoes. Other stratovolcanoes you might have heard of are Mount Hood in Oregon and Mount St. Helens in Washington.

Mount Fuji

Paricutín

Cinder Cone Volcanoes

Cinder cones are another common type of volcano. These volcanoes usually start out small, but they can quickly build up into a large cone. As lava explodes from the central vent, it breaks into small pieces that fall as cinders around the opening. The material forms a cone-shaped mountain. The Paricutín (pah-ree-koo-TEEN) volcano in Mexico is one of the most famous cinder cone volcanoes.

It's a Fact

Before the eruption of Paricutín, which began in 1943, a Mexican farmer noticed some strange happenings in his cornfield. He heard rumbling noises and saw smoke coming out of the soil. The next day, a cinder cone had started to form in the field. That was the beginning of the volcano. During its nine-year lifespan, it built a 1,345-foot-high cone (410 meters) with vast lava fields around its base.

Shield Volcanoes

Some of the largest volcanoes in the world are shield volcanoes. Unlike stratovolcanoes and cinder cones, shield volcanoes are wide and flat. Shield volcanoes are made almost entirely of lava that flows outward, forming a broad shape somewhat like a warrior's shield. The lava spreads out over a large area and cools into gently rippling sheets of rock.

Most of the Hawaiian Islands are shield volcanoes.

Mauna Loa (MAW-nuh LOH-uh), on the island of Hawaii, is the world's largest volcano. It rises more than five miles from the floor of the Pacific Ocean. Mauna Loa's base is 60 miles (97 kilometers) long and 30 miles (48 kilometers) wide. This volcano is so big that it "houses" another major volcano. The Kilauea (kee-luh-WEH-uh) volcano sits on the southeastern slope of Mauna Loa.

Mauna Loa

15

Three Types of Volcanoes

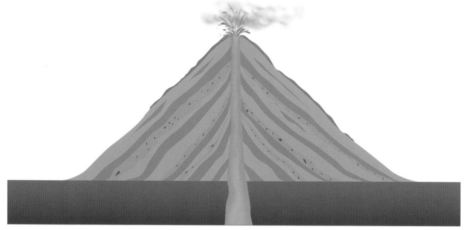

stratovolcano

cinder cone volcano

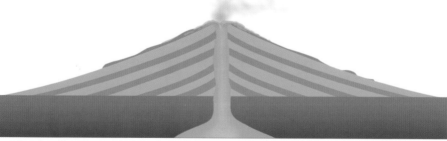

shield volcano

Sometimes the magma chamber of a volcano almost completely empties because of an eruption. When that happens, the empty chamber can no longer support the weight above. The top of the volcano collapses and forms a circular depression called a **caldera** (kal-DAIR-uh). Caldera is the Spanish word for a cauldron, or pot. Crater Lake in Oregon is a caldera that has filled with water. It is about 2,000 feet (610 meters) deep. That makes it the deepest freshwater lake in North America.

Where else can you find calderas? There are calderas on the shield volcanoes of the Galápagos Islands. Calderas can be found even in outer space. The Olympus Mons caldera on Mars is almost 15 miles (24.14 kilometers) high and more than 300 miles (482.80 kilometers) wide at its base. Imagine how high this volcano must have been before it collapsed!

Crater Lake in Oregon

CHAPTER 3

WHEN VOLCANOES ERUPT

Scientists give names to the different types of volcanic eruptions. Geologists call the most explosive kind of volcanic eruption a Peléean (puh-LAY-yuhn) eruption. The name comes from the 1902 eruption of Mont Pelée (mon puh-LAY) on the island of Martinique in the West Indies.

Early in the morning of May 8, Mont Pelée exploded with four thundering blasts.

Suddenly, a pyroclastic flow swept down the volcano. Volcanologists estimate the temperatures of the flow to have reached 1,300 degrees Fahrenheit (704 degrees Celsius).

It's a Fact

Mont Pelée destroyed the capital city of Saint Pierre. Nearly 30,000 people were killed. The only survivors were a prisoner in a dungeon and a person at the far end of town. The flow burned ships in the harbor and boiled the seawater, killing masses of sea organisms.

the ruins of Saint Pierre

Scientists call the least violent kind of eruption a Hawaiian eruption. In this kind of eruption, lava streams out of several vents and gradually forms a shield volcano. In a Strombolian eruption, gas periodically escapes from the magma, sending out volcanic material that forms a cinder cone. A Vulcanian eruption is caused when thickened or solidified magma plugs up the central vent. The result is a buildup of pressure that forces the magma to blast out.

It's a Fact

The word *Strombolian* comes from the Stromboli volcano on an island near Italy. This volcano has been erupting almost continuously for at least 2,400 years.

Stromboli volcano erupting

FAMOUS VOLCANOES

Read about a few of the most famous volcanoes in history.

Mount Vesuvius

(vuh-SOO-vee-uhs)

Where: Italy

When: August 24, 79 C.E.

What happened: Nobody saw this one coming. People who lived near this volcano thought it was extinct. They were very wrong. When Mount Vesuvius erupted, ash and lava buried the towns of Pompeii (pahm-PAY), Herculaneum (hur-kyuh-LAY-nee-uhm), and Stabiae (stah-BEE-ay).

Deaths: About 2,000 people

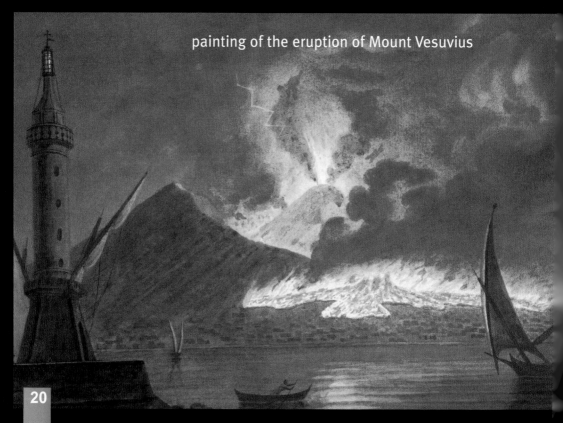

painting of the eruption of Mount Vesuvius

Naples, Italy, a city of more than one million people, is only 7 miles (11 kilometers) from Mount Vesuvius. People live on the lower slopes of the volcano.

PRIMARY SOURCE

Here's an eyewitness account of the eruption of Mount Vesuvius, written by an author named Pliny the Younger.

"Ashes were already falling, not as yet very thickly. I looked round: a dense black cloud was coming up behind us, spreading over the earth like a flood. We had scarcely sat down to rest when darkness fell, not the dark of a moonless or cloudy night, but as if the lamp had been put out in a closed room. You could hear the shrieks of women, the wailing infants, and the shouting of men. . ."

Krakatoa

Where: A tiny island in Indonesia in the South Pacific

When: 1883

What happened: Krakatoa had a powerful eruption. The blast was so loud that people 3,000 miles (4,839 kilometers) away heard it!

Deaths: Since no one lived on Krakatoa, no one died there. But the eruption caused huge waves up to 120 feet (37 meters) high. Those waves, called **tsunamis** (soo-NAH-meez), crashed into the nearby islands of Java and Sumatra. About 36,000 people drowned in the flooded villages.

It's a Fact

Following the 1883 eruption of Krakatoa, an enormous cloud of ash blocked out the sun for more than two days. The wind carried volcanic ash 50 miles (80 kilometers) into the atmosphere. The ash spread out all over the world.

▲ 1883 eruption of Krakatoa

Mount St. Helens

Where: Washington State, United States

When: 1980

What happened: First the volcano rumbled with earthquakes. Soon the peak grew a large bulge where magma was collecting under the surface. Finally, a large, spectacular eruption blew the top off the volcano. The blast snapped trees as if they were matchsticks and covered the landscape with ash. The pyroclastic explosion melted the ice cap that covered the top of the volcano. The rushing water tore down the slopes carrying with it volcanic ash and other debris. It will take 100 years before a mature forest once again covers the slopes of Mount St. Helens.

Deaths: 57 people

▼ This car was destroyed by the 1980 eruption of Mount St. Helens.

Mount Pinatubo

Where: The Philippines

When: 1991

What happened: Mount Pinatubo (PEE-nah-TOO-boh) erupted in a powerful blast ten times larger than the eruption of Mount St. Helens. A giant ash cloud shot 22 miles (35 kilometers) into the sky, and hot blasts burned the countryside. Due to timely warnings, a large-scale evacuation of 78,000 people took place, saving thousands of lives. Following the eruption, heavy rains caused widespread avalanches of volcanic ash and other material.

Deaths: About 700 people

▼ 1991 eruption of Mount Pinatubo

Famous Volcanic Eruptions

Volcano	Country	Date of Eruption	Description
Mount Vesuvius	Italy	79 C.E.	Volcanic ash buried the towns of Herculaneum, Pompeii, and Stabiae. Ruins were not uncovered for about 1,700 years.
Mount Etna	Sicily	1669	Eruption killed about 20,000 people. Europe's tallest active volcano (about 11,000 feet or 3,352.8 meters high)
Mount Tambora	Indonesia	1815	Sent more than 1,500,000 tons of dust into the atmosphere. Reduced sunlight and temperatures, resulting in "the year without a summer"
Mauna Loa	Hawaii, United States	1855–56	The world's largest volcano—about 30,000 feet (9,100 meters) above the ocean floor
Krakatoa	Indonesia	1883	Caused sea waves about 120 feet (37 meters) high that drowned about 36,000 people on nearby islands
Mont Pelée	Martinique	1902	Killed about 30,000 people in minutes
Paricutín	Mexico	1943–52	The 1943 eruption built a cinder cone about 500 feet (152.4 meters) high in six days.
Mount St. Helens	Washington, United States	1980	Explosion blasted away the peak. Caused hundreds of millions of dollars of damage to the surrounding area
El Chichón	Mexico	1982	Killed about 2,000 people. Released a cloud of dust and sulfur dioxide into the atmosphere
Nevado del Ruiz	Colombia	1985	Eruption triggered mudslides and floods that killed about 25,000 people.
Mount Unzen	Japan	1991	The worst volcanic disaster in Japan's history. Resulted in about 15,000 deaths
Mount Pinatubo	Philippines	1991	The eruption was 10 times larger than the 1980 eruption of Mount St. Helens. Released 20 million tons (18 million metric tons) of sulfur dioxide into the atmosphere.
Mount Ruapehu	New Zealand	1996	No fatalities, due to satellite warning system

The Good and Bad of Volcanoes

ew forces of nature are as destructive as volcanoes. Volcanic eruptions can wipe out entire cities, villages, towns, and their inhabitants. Some volcanic eruptions have caused tsunamis that slammed onto land, washing away everything in their paths. Other eruptions have spewed ash high into the atmosphere, affecting the world's weather.

In 1815, the eruption of Mount Tambora in Indonesia spread ash clouds worldwide. The ash clouds lowered temperatures by blocking out the sunlight. As a result, the spring and summer of 1816 were unusually cold. In June, July, and August heavy snows fell in parts of North America. The year of 1816 became known as "the year without a summer."

✔ POINT

Picture It

Imagine "a year without a summer" due to a volcanic eruption. Draw a picture of what would happen to summer crops.

Can anything good come from a volcanic eruption? The answer is yes. Over time, lava fields turn into rich soil that is ideal for farming. Farmers grow grapes on the slopes of Mount Vesuvius. On the slopes of the Agung (AH-goong) volcano in Bali, Indonesia, farmers plant fields of rice. Pineapples, sugarcane, and coffee beans also grow well in volcanic soil.

Some countries, including the United States, Mexico, and New Zealand, use **geothermal energy**, meaning "energy from the Earth." Hot magma near places of high volcanic activity heats water that is underground, turning some of it into steam. The heated water and steam are piped into power plants where they are used to produce electricity. In Iceland, underground water is so hot that it is piped directly into homes as a source of heat.

pineapple field in Hawaii

CHAPTER 6

PREDICTING VOLCANIC ERUPTIONS

How can we tell when a volcano might erupt? Volcanologists look for telltale signs of volcanic activity. Before an eruption, there is often an increase in the amount of gases that escape from the magma.

Volcanologists recorded an increase in the amount of sulfur dioxide gas escaping from Mount Pinatubo months before the 1991 eruption.

Earthquakes are one of the most important clues to an impending eruption. This is because rising magma often places pressure on the volcano, making cracks and setting off small earthquakes. Before the eruption of Mount Pinatubo, earthquakes increased in intensity.

It's a Fact

In 1994, scientists used a robot to explore an active volcano in Alaska. The robot, named Dante II, was able to gather valuable data. Then it damaged one of its legs, fell, and had to be rescued by helicopter.

This volcanologist is taking a gas sample near a volcanic vent.

Scientists also use satellite images to predict volcanic eruptions. Such long-range images taken from space show changes in Earth's surface temperatures. By comparing the images of a volcano taken over time, scientists can track increases in temperature. Chances are that a great increase in temperature means that the volcano is heating up and getting ready to "blow."

Predicting the eruption of a volcano is not an exact science. Volcanologists have many tools that help them make predictions, yet their forecasts are not always accurate. Some volcanoes give out warning signs; others do not.

▲ This NASA photo shows the grayish-white ash and mud deposits from the 1991 eruption of Mount Pinatubo. At the time this image was taken, water filled the caldera of the volcano.

THEY MADE A DIFFERENCE

French scientists Maurice and Katia Krafft are among the best known volcanologists. This married couple worked together studying and photographing volcanoes throughout the world. They were most interested in pyroclastic eruptions. Sadly, the couple died in 1991 when the pyroclastic flow from Mount Unzen, Japan, swept them away.

CONCLUSION

Today, scientists help reveal the secrets of volcanoes, providing clues to their inner workings. We know where volcanoes are located. We know the kinds of eruptions that occur. Volcanologists not only study volcanoes. They also try to predict their eruptions. That's not an easy task. Why? Some volcanoes refuse to give up all their secrets.

CAREERS IN SCIENCE

Would you like to become a volcanologist? Be prepared to focus on math and science in high school. Then major in science at the college level. You will need to study several sciences, the most important of which is geology. With a Ph.D. in geology— an advanced degree—you might work for the U.S. Geological Survey. This agency operates volcano observatories in Hawaii, Washington, California, Wyoming, and Alaska.

▼ A volcanologist in protective clothing takes measurements of a lava flow.

GLOSSARY

caldera   **(kal-DAIR-uh) a large circular depression formed when the top of a volcano collapses** (page 17)

crust   **(KRUST) the outermost layer of Earth's surface** (page 4)

geothermal energy   **(jee-oh-THER-mul EH-ner-jee) energy that comes from heat inside Earth** (page 27)

hot spot   **(HAHT SPAHT) an underground area of super-hot rock** (page 12)

lava   **(LAH-vuh) melted rock that has erupted from a volcano onto Earth's surface** (page 2)

magma   **(MAG-muh) melted rock found inside Earth** (page 4)

plate tectonics   **(PLATE tek-TAH-niks) a scientific theory that Earth's surface is made up of about 10 huge plates and 6 smaller plates that fit together like a huge jigsaw puzzle** (page 5)

pyroclastic flow   **(py-roh-KLAS-tik FLOH) a tall column of pyroclastic materials and gases that collapses and races down the slopes of the volcano at dangerous speeds** (page 8)

tsunami   **(soo-NAH-mee) a giant tidal wave, caused by a volcano or earthquake** (page 22)

vent   **(VENT) a weak spot in Earth's crust through which magma can rise to the surface** (page 6)

volcano   **(vahl-KAY-noh) any opening on Earth where material from inside the planet makes its way to the surface** (page 6)

INDEX